The Seattle Totem Pole

The Seattle totem pole represents one of the most unusual types of craftsmanship in the world. Carved only in the Pacific Northwest, notably by the Tlingit of southeastern Alaska and the Haida and Tsimshian of western Canada, totem poles can rise to heights of sixty feet: vertical legends of the tribe embodied in ravens, whales, frogs, and other creatures.

Seattle's totem pole came from the Tlingit village of Tongass. The original pole belonged to a Tlingit lineage of the Raven clan, known in English as the Kininook family. It was erected in front of the lineage house in honor of a woman called Chief-of-All-Women, who drowned in the Nass River while on her way to visit a sister who was ill. As was customary, her brothers and sisters and other lineage members planned a memorial for her. They hired a carver and told him the stories they wanted represented on a pole. When the pole was completed, the lineage organized a potlatch and the pole was erected in the name of Chief-of-All-Women. It is one of few poles dedicated to a woman; most were carved in honor of deceased chiefs who traditionally were men.

In 1899 a group of Seattle businessmen chartered a ship for a tour in the south of Alaska. On their way home to Seattle they stopped at Tongass, which appeared to be deserted. They did not know that all the able-bodied men were out salmon fishing and that the women were away working in the canneries which processed the fish for shipment south. Only the elderly and small children remained in the village.

Admiring the unusual poles, the men decided to take one back to Seattle as a souvenir. Completely disregarding the fact that the Indians owned the pole and that it was a memorial to an ancestor, they went ashore, sawed it down, and floated it to their ship. In doing so, they broke the beak on the bottom figure, and since no one later remembered the original design, the beak was not reconstructed in its traditional shape.

Totem poles in the village of Tongass, Alaska, ca. 1899. Pole at far right was removed to Seattle in that year. Courtesy National Archives, Records of the Fish and Wildlife Service (22-FA-218)

Although the sponsors of the touring party were eventually fined for the theft, the pole nevertheless remained to become a treasured landmark in Seattle. It was placed in Pioneer Square in an official dedication on October 18, 1899, where it stood until damaged by fire in October of 1938. When it was removed for inspection, it was found to be too greatly damaged by dry rot for repair. In order not to lose this famed historic artwork, familiar to pioneers and newcomers alike, the Seattle City Council and the Park Board began to investigate the possibility of having it copied.

In 1938 the United States Forest Service was directing the restoration of poles by native craftsmen in southeastern Alaska. When the regional forester in charge of the work heard of the damage to the Seattle pole, he offered to undertake duplication of the pole by Tlingit carvers working in his program. Since no carvers were available in Seattle, the pole was shipped to the Forest Service workshop in Saxman, two miles from Ketchikan, where the copy was made under the direction of Charles Brown, a skilled Tlingit craftsman. His father, William H. Brown, gave the final adzed surface texturing to the pole. The chief helpers were James Starfish, Robert Harris, William Andrews, and James Andrews, all Tlingit carvers, some closely related to the lineage to which the pole belonged.

Unveiling the totem pole in Pioneer Square, Seattle, 18 October 1899. Courtesy Photo Collection, University of Washington Library

Charles Brown, head carver for the new Seattle pole, and his father, standing beside the old Seattle totem pole at Saxman. Courtesy Photo Collection, University of Washington Library

Carvers at work, ca. 1938. From left: Felix Young, Peter Jones, Walter Young, and James Peele, who donated the cedar for the new Seattle pole. Note native type of adzes with which most of the carving was done. Each workman makes his own adzes to suit his style of carving. Photograph by Ray C. Snow, courtesy Photo Collection, University of Washington Library

The tree itself came from Kina Cove, an arm of Kasaan Bay in southeastern Alaska, and was seventy feet long with a thirty-inch-wide top. More durable than hemlock, from which the original was made, the timber for the new pole was red cedar. This cedar was graciously donated for the Seattle pole by James Peele, a Haida who had selected the tree to carve a duplicate of a pole for his father, Chief Sonihat of Old Kasaan. The log was towed to the workshop at Saxman, where it was cut to fifty-six feet in length, the bark and sapwood removed, and the pole trimmed to symmetrical shape, ready for the carvers. The bottom of the pole was four and one-half feet in diameter with a six-foot base, making the carved section fifty feet long.

Native types of long-handled adzes and knives fitted with steel blades were used throughout construction. After the head carver had marked out and roughed in the figures, other carvers worked in the main outlines. As many as ten men worked on the pole for short intervals during the early stages of the work, taking great care to copy the body curves, postures, and facial expressions of the figures on the original pole. Older men, with long experience in carving, gave advice and, using an adze, put the delicate and intricate details on the pole. The surface of the pole was finished with a pattern of regularly placed adze marks, an effect that could be achieved with no other tool.

When the carving was completed, many coats of wood preservative were applied. Since the early carvers had devised no methods for preserving wood and used paint only for emphasis of detail, the main body of the poles was left the natural wood. Over the years the original Seattle pole had been covered with successive coats of paint in decidedly non-Tlingit colors and patterns in an attempt to preserve it. The new pole, however, was painted with native colors of black, red, and bluish green, to resemble the original at the time of its removal from Tongass. The brick red of the ochre and the bluish green shades of the copper paints of native manufacture were duplicated as closely as possible in commercial paint, since the native paints, whose binder was the oil chewed out of salmon or herring eggs, were no longer being made.

Three months of work transformed the tree into the finished pole, ready for shipment to Seattle. Because the timber for the pole had come from Forest Service land, and the carvers had been paid by the government, a special act of Congress was required to transfer ownership from the United States Forest Service to the city of Seattle. In Seattle the pole was raised in Pioneer Square where the old pole had stood, and was acknowledged by speeches and a gathering of businessmen and representatives of the mayor's office.

Loading the new pole on S.S. Tanana in Saxman for shipment to Seattle, April 1940. Courtesy Photo Collection, University of Washington Library

An artist's view of Pioneer Square during the 1880s. Courtesy Photo
Collection, University of Washington Library

The fifty-foot imposing column, centrally placed, has added
greatly to the distinctive character and charm of Pioneer Square. The
land now occupied by the pole was, in the 1870s, a wide open area
known as Occidental Square. It was the lively scene of circuses,
impromptu games, and informal gatherings. In 1889 an overheated
glue pot in a basement carpentry shop on Front Street (now First
Avenue) set off the city's great fire, which decimated the many
wooden buildings and left the streets surrounding the Square in
desolation. The rebuilding, which began immediately, included a
small park for flowers in the middle of the Square. The triangular plot
of grass remained empty for several years, until the arrival of the
totem pole in 1899, and eventually benches for people to wait for the
street cars and a watering trough for horses were added. The Square
over the years has matured into a gracious and comfortable public
park.

The new triangle with its single tree, in the Pioneer Square district rebuilt after the great fire of 1889. Courtesy Photo Collection, University of Washington Library

The totem pole, an established ornament in the Square in the early 1900s.
Courtesy Photo Collection, University of Washington Library

A modern view of the Square and totem pole, 1979.

Legends Symbolized

Totem poles are always "read" from the top downward. The topmost figure identifies the owner; on the Seattle pole this figure is Raven. In his beak he holds the crescent moon. Other characters on the pole are a woman holding her frog child, the woman's frog husband, Mink, Raven, and Whale with a seal in his mouth. And, finally, at the base of the pole is Raven-at-the-Head-of-Nass, also called Grandfather of Raven.

Three main legends belonging to the lineage are illustrated on the pole. The first is represented by the topmost and the lowest figures and is the tale of the ancient mythological era of Tlingit life.

One day Raven decided to get the daylight for the world. He started at the mouth of the Nass River. Near there he met a party of half-humans fishing. He asked them for food. They jeered him, saying, "We know you are only the trickster Raven." Raven walked on up the river. When he came to the Supernatural's house he asked to see the chief. The slaves turned him away as they also recognized him as Trickster.

Raven retired to a nearby lake and sat down to think. He knew that the chief's daughter came to the lake for her drinking water. He turned himself into a bit of dirt and floated on the lake. Soon the princess came with her drinking basket and her slave. She dipped a basket of water and saw the bit of dirt, which she promptly threw out. Raven sat down and thought some more. He then turned himself into a hemlock needle, which is almost transparent in the water, and waited. The next time the princess came down for a drink he floated into the basket and she did not notice him. She drank the needle and swallowed it. It was soon apparent that she was pregnant. The chief called his wisest men, but they could give him no explanation. She gave birth to a son, Raven.

The baby grew fast and was soon crawling about. His grandfather thought a great deal of him and let him play with everything he wanted. One day little Raven cried for the box containing the moon and would not be quieted until it was given to him. He played with it on the floor for awhile, then broke the box open and the moon rose and floated out through the smokehole into the sky, where it has been ever since.

Later Raven cried for the box in which the sun was stored. He cried for a very long time until he became ill. Finally the grandfather said, "Bring my child here." They handed Raven to his grandfather. Then his grandfather said to him, "My grandchild, I am giving you the last thing I have in the world." So he gave him the box containing the sun. Little Raven rolled it around on the floor, awaiting his chance. When the smokehole was open he picked up the box, changed into bird form, and flew away. He was covered with soot as he flew through the smokehole (and so all ravens are now black).

He walked down the Nass River and again met the animal-people fishing on the shore. He again asked them for food and they again mocked him. He then opened the box and let the sunlight out. The animal-people were so frightened that they tried to escape. Those dressed in animal skins ran into the woods and became land animals. Those in bird feathers flew into the trees and became birds and those in fish skins dove into the water and changed into fish. Only those who were naked stayed on land and became people.

Raven-at-the-Head-of-Nass, bottom figure on the Seattle totem pole. Courtesy Photo Collection, University of Washington Library

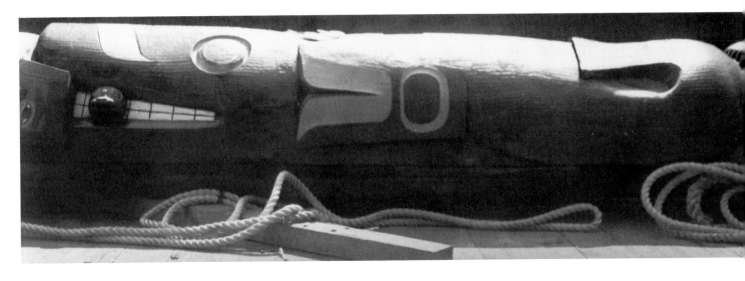

Killerwhale with a seal in his mouth. Courtesy Photo Collection, University of Washington Library

A second tale symbolized on the pole is another episode in the adventures of Raven, the trickster-culture hero. This Raven stands on the tail of a blackfish, or whale, carved head down, with prominent dorsal fin and the blowhole shown as a face with open mouth. Pectoral fins are carved on either side of the blackfish, and he holds a seal in his mouth.

Raven was always hungry. One day he was standing on the beach and he saw a whale. That gave him an idea. He gathered firewood and stones with which to strike fire and the next time the whale rose he dove into its mouth. In its stomach he built a fire. When the whale swallowed fish he cooked it over his fire. If there were more fish than he could eat he cut them up and hung them about to dry. When he did not get enough fish to satisfy his voracious appetite he cut slices of fat from the whale's stomach.

Finally he became tired of his journeying about, so he cut out the whale's heart and killed him. When the whale was dead, Raven began to sing, "Let the whale go ashore. Let the whale go ashore on a long sandy beach." They then drifted ashore and Raven again sang, "Let someone cut the whale open and let me out." People living nearby had seen the whale drifting ashore and came down to cut it up for oil and meat. When they heard Raven singing they cut the whale open and he escaped. He was very dirty and covered with grease. He flew away and preened himself so he is now very sleek and glossy. Raven came back later and frightened the people away from the whale by telling them that they would all die if they ate it. He stayed until he had consumed all the meat and oil himself. Then he set off for further adventures.

This is an often-told tale. In one version Raven tried to steal food from Whale and was swallowed by mistake. When Raven complained of hunger, Whale told him to cut out pieces of fat, taking care not to touch his heart. Raven, in his greed, did not heed the caution and killed his host. According to another version of the tale, Mink accompanied Raven on this venture, hence his appearance on the pole.

The third tale on the Seattle pole is illustrated by the figures under the top raven. They are a woman holding her frog child, head downward, his little legs sticking up just under her chin. Below, also head downward, is her frog husband. One of the crests owned by the Raven clan is Frog, and there are many tales of the marriages and adventures of clan ancestors with frogs.

A young woman made some derogatory remarks about frogs. One of them heard her and changed himself into a personable young man who then courted her. She married him and was taken to his home. Many young people were there and she was very happy until she accidentally discovered that their home was under a lake and her husband and his people were frogs. She then sent her children to her human father's home. When the little frogs came into the house they were chased away. They kept coming back, and their grandfather began to suspect something, so he sent his human nephews to watch where the frogs went. They saw his daughter sitting in the middle of the lake with her frog husband and children. The nephews told their uncle what they had seen. They then drained the lake, killing her frog husband and rescuing the daughter and her frog children. She had eaten so much frog food, however, that she did not live long. Her children, though they behaved for a long time like frogs, finally became completely human and never went back to their frog home.

Mink is the only figure on the pole for which there are no tales, although he is occasionally mentioned in the company of Raven. Mink was a guardian spirit, or spirit helper, of a Tlingit ancestor who was a shaman. When a young man determined to train as a shaman, he isolated himself from the village, took frequent baths, fasted and dried himself with spruce boughs or devil's club branches to remove any contamination of the human smell about himself. He then concentrated on the spiritual, hoping that a spirit would appear to him. And so it happened with this particular ancestor as a young man: he acquired Mink as his spirit helper. When he attended a patient he danced, sang, and called his spirit helper to diagnose the illness. The spirit helper revealed whether the patient had lost his or her soul or whether a foreign object had been injected into the patient's body. At that point the shaman could try to remedy the situation and cure the patient. Because men in solitude, preparing to become shamans, never thereafter revealed their experiences, their visions, or the nature of their guardians, we have no details of these spirit helpers in legend.

There are many "totem poles" in the Puget Sound area. They have been carved by white men or by native Americans unfamiliar with their tribal history; many were made to order for particular locations or purposes. Their designs do not refer to lineage-owned tales or crests. A number of poles, carved by a Puget Sound Indian, are carved on all four sides of square timbers; one even includes a likeness of Franklin D. Roosevelt. Today, the Seattle totem pole is one of the few poles in a public setting carved by native craftsmen to honor a deceased relative and illustrating the myths and events of a specific lineage. The myths and legends of the totem figures on the Seattle pole described here are just a few of many myths owned by the lineage of Chief-of-All-Women.

Frog Woman with her child and husband.

Northwest Coast Totem Pole Art

The carving of totem poles was brought to a high stage of development by the native peoples of the Pacific Northwest. Their sculpture and relief carving in wood, stone, and bone ranged from tiny ornaments to massive works of heroic proportions. Single sculptured figures eight feet tall and spectacular carved totem poles as high as sixty feet graced their villages.

Decorative carving was characteristic of the entire North Pacific coast and a well-established art form by the eighteenth century. Explorers commented on the elaborate carving that adorned the houses, both inside and out, and the beautifully executed household utensils and furniture. They collected baskets, boxes, woven hats, blankets, and tools that are now housed in museums in Europe, the Soviet Union, South Africa, and the United States. There is no mention of tall carved poles in their reports. Totem poles can be traced to the latter half of the 1880s, however, when metal cutting tools acquired from European traders facilitated the work of carving large timbers. Alejandro Malaspina, an eighteenth-century explorer, visited Yakutat Bay in Tlingit territory with an artist who drew pictures of carved posts decorated in the style of the boxes and posts identified from this period. A large wolf holding a burial box on his knees is a typical figure.

The moist, heavily wooded coastal area provided the peoples of the Northwest with readily available large trees. The size, durability, and straight grain of cedar made it especially desirable for carving. Sound timber close to the beach was plentiful and furnished ample wood for houses, canoes, household furniture, implements, and tools. These were carved with great skill and artistry in pre-European times when shell, beaver incisors, and stone were the only materials available for cutting blades. The same painstaking and artistic work was done on knife handles, halibut hooks, and fish clubs as on large canoes and elaborate equipment for ceremonial use, and the same carved and painted designs decorated them.

When Captain Cook first made contact with the Indians, he found them using a few bits of iron and wondered where it came from. There has been speculation that the Indians learned to utilize iron from ancient junks from the Orient, wrecked on their shores. Another theory holds that small pieces of iron were traded down the Alaska coast, with the source being Siberia. The Indians themselves, however, offered no answers and have no legends of where the iron originated.

By the mid 1700s explorers and fur traders were exchanging pieces of iron for sea otter skins. The Indians fashioned iron into blades for their adzes and draw knives, and carving flourished as never before. Larger canoes and finer houses were built, along with a greater number and variety of boxes, dishes, and decorative articles. Axes, introduced by the traders at about the same time, were a great help in felling and trimming trees and the tall totem pole made its appearance.

The Eagle grave memorial, which stood in the old village of Howkan, is one of the most stately and impressive of Alaskan sculptures. It is five and one-half feet tall. The feathers and the iris of the eye were originally painted black and the beak and feet yellow, but only fragments of the paint now adhere to the wood. In the grass beside the pole are two land-otter figures representing drowned men transformed into otters in mythology. Photograph by J. E. Thwaites, courtesy Photo Collection, University of Washington Library

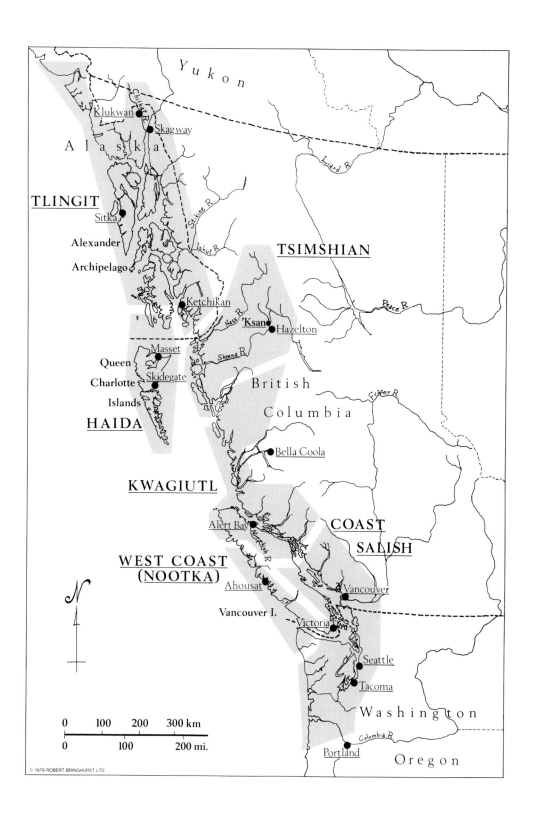

Y u k o n

Chilkat R.

Klukwan

Skagway

A l a s k a

Liard R.

TLINGIT

Sitka

St. kine R.

Alexander

TSIMSHIAN

Iskut R.

Archipelago

Peace R.

Ketchikan

Nass R.

'Ksan

Hazelton

Masset

Skeena R.

Queen

Charlotte

Skidegate

British

Islands

Columbia

HAIDA

Fraser R.

Bella Coola

KWAGIUTL

COAST

Alert Bay

SALISH

WEST COAST

Nootka R.

(NOOTKA)

Ahousat

Vancouver

Vancouver I.

Victoria

Seattle

Tacoma

N

W a s h i n g t o n

0   100   200   300 km

0   100   200 mi.

Columbia R.

Portland   O r e g o n

© 1979 ROBERT BRINGHURST LTD

Around the middle of the nineteenth century there were probably thousands of tall poles in existence, all made within a period of about fifty years. Skidegate, on the Queen Charlotte Islands, had dozens of tall poles facing the water and many more around the houses back from the beach. Kasaan, on Prince of Wales Island, had at least one pole in front of every house in the village. In 1920 when an anthropologist visited the abandoned village of Tongass, he counted 120 carved columns. These were mainly fifteen- to twenty-foot house posts and memorial or grave markers. Most were still standing, though a few had rotted and fallen. In the dryer interior of British Columbia poles had survived somewhat longer.

When they were first carved in the early part of the century, the totem poles were set against the front of the house with an entrance cut through the base of the pole; later they were placed free of the house fronts, facing the beach, as many as three or four in front of a single house. The sides and front were the only carved portions of the pole; the back was frequently hollowed out into a shell. Poles were placed where guests, arriving in the village by canoe, could view the carved front.

Totem poles in Skidegate Village, Queen Charlotte Islands, ca. 1878. Photograph by James Swan, courtesy Photo Collection, University of Washington Library

Poles adorning Old Kasaan village. This photograph is an enlargement of a stereoptican slide by Underwood and Underwood, dated between 1898 and 1904. Courtesy Photo Collection, University of Washington Library

The raising and dedication of a totem pole was always an elaborate affair, worthy of a potlatch of gifts and feasting. Guests invited to the potlatch dug the hole and set the pole in place, while their hosts explained the figures on the pole, most of which illustrated tales of past tribal events. The legends were dramatized in songs and dances, and the performers wore costumes and carved masks. Thus the success of the potlatch demanded and encouraged dramatic and artistic talents: composers, singers, actors, drummers, and dancers, as well as a stage director. The hosts offered food, and secured their reputations by the extravagance of their gifts.

Missionaries were scornful of the potlatch and of the poles themselves, interpreting them as heathen symbols. They destroyed some poles and discouraged this style of carving. In addition, white frontiersmen developing the fish and timber industries in the area found the potlatch wasteful and heathen and the men involved in the intricate and time-consuming preparations unreliable at work. In this climate, around the turn of the century, it is not surprising that government officials in the United States and Canada voted to outlaw the practice, which nearly ended the carving of poles and masks and other works of art. Early in the 1950s, when this ban was removed, a revival of interest in their heritage among native Americans again brought the potlatch into public view.

Traditionally, the design of the totem pole was inspired by and referred symbolically to the incidents described in the mythology and legendary history of the people. Many of these tales are familiar throughout the Northwest Coast area, and different versions of each are known and related, even in the same community of villages. Other tales are the special property of a group of people who consider themselves descended from a common clan ancestor, and these stories relate experiences and adventures of members of the group. Stories are best known by those to whom they belong, since they are never fully told to outsiders.

The Tlingit, Haida, and Tsimshian all have matrilineal clan organization, tracing their descent only through their mothers. Their poles thus belong to a group (called a lineage) of brothers and sisters and the children of sisters. A man and his wife belong to different lineages and the children take the name of their mother's lineage. Many Northwest Coast lineages are related to each other and form what is called a clan, sharing a name and crests or totems. Every Tlingit and Haida, for example, belongs to either the Raven or the Eagle clan; the Tsimshian have four clan divisions: the Ravens, Eagles, Wolves, and Killerwhales. Each division owns tales of their origin and ancestors as well as tangible fishing sites, berry fields, home locations, and hunting grounds.

The figures carved on the pole are drawn from these ancestral tales of lineages. Since many of the characters in native legend could perform marvelous feats such as changing themselves from human beings into frogs, birds, or hemlock needles at will, the method of depicting them involved symbolizing their supernatural attributes. The artists sought readily recognizable qualities by which to represent the mythical animals whose deeds and adventures belonged to a heroic world, and the form and style became highly conventionalized.

Since a supernatural being could appear in both human and animal form, the figures often combined the characteristics of both. One of the mythological beings about which there are many tales is Raven. Members of the Raven clan believed that their ancestors witnessed certain of Raven's exploits and they therefore could claim the right to tell the tales and illustrate them in carvings and paintings. Sometimes Raven is shown as a bird with straight beak and wings; he also can have human arms and legs and wear a chief's hat. In one carving he has been given both bird's wings and human arms and hands, but he is recognizable by his straight beak.

The Thunderbird was also widely believed in as a supernatural being. He was always depicted as a bird with large, turned-down beak. When he was hungry he went to the sea, picked up a whale in his talons, and took it to the top of a mountain to eat. Thunder came from the throb of the bird's wings as he flew and lightening from the flash of his eyes. (Occasionally the whale is also depicted, and it is said that whale bones can still be seen on the tops of mountains.)

Aside from Raven and Thunderbird, other characters frequently appearing in Northwest Coast carving and sculpture are Bear, Wolf, Eagle, Blackfish or Killerwhale, Salmon, Frog, and Beaver. Some generalizations will help to identify the various creatures.

Beaks identify birds or their anthropomorphic forms. Raven's beak is straight, Eagle's and Thunderbird's curved, and Hawk's turns into his mouth. A raven's beak on a human face represents Raven, the hero, in human form. On the Seattle totem pole Raven is depicted as a bird, carrying the moon in his beak. On a pole in Wrangell, Alaska, illustrating the same story, he is given human ears to establish his supernatural character and the sun disk surrounds his face. On this same pole his mother is shown in bird form though the story relates that she was human. His grandfather is shown in bird form on both poles and is described as an anthropomorphic being.

Killerwhale can be symbolized simply by the portrayal of a dorsal fin; his other distinguishing marks are a blunt face, sharp teeth, round eye, and white band across the nose, as well as the small face on the blowhole. Artists do not clearly distinguish the various species of whale, killerwhale, and blackfish in their art.

Mink is not often illustrated. On the pole in Seattle his slender, long tail, turned up on his stomach, is the chief identifying mark; otherwise he could be mistaken for a bear. Bear and Wolf are not always easily distinguishable, since both have long, narrow snouts, sharp teeth, and sharp claws.

On the other hand, many figures are easy to identify, whether on a spoon handle or a fifty-foot totem pole. One of these is Frog, usually carved realistically and painted green with white or black markings to correspond to the animal's natural coloring. Beaver can be recognized by two large incisors and a paddle-shaped, crosshatched tail.

Raven on Seattle pole, showing the straight beak. Courtesy Photo Collection, University of Washington Library

Raven with sun disk around his face, at Wrangell, Alaska. From top: spruce root hat, creator in human-raven form, sun box, Raven with sun halo, Raven's mother, Raven in bird form, Tide Watcher. Courtesy Photo Collection, University of Washington Library

An animal's ears are stylized and placed to either side of the top of the head, while the ears of an ordinary human being are anatomically correct as to shape and placement. A human face with these stylized animal ears usually portrays some being with both animal and human properties.

Eyes are extensively used in native carving. They may symbolize hip, shoulder, or other joints, nostrils, the inner ear, the blowhole of a whale, or the palm of a hand. They are sometimes elaborated into faces for decorative effect. The eye embodies the concept of the life or vital principle: in the ear, it symbolizes the faculty of hearing; in the nostril, a keen sense of smell; in the joints, vitality or body movement. On the Seattle pole, faces in profile are carved and painted in the ears of the bottom figure, Raven's grandfather, typifying the all-pervading powers of this mysterious being.

In placing his design on the article he is decorating, the artist follows certain traditional principles of arrangement. Since symbols are emphasized at the expense of less essential parts of an image, most body parts of figures can be eliminated. Faces and heads are often very large and limbs small or even left out altogether. No attempt is made to show perspective or relative size, or to achieve anatomical accuracy. Where several characters are illustrated, such as on the side of a box or totem pole, they are telescoped into each other and so arranged as to cover the whole space available. To satisfy aesthetic requirements the artist does not hesitate to take his subject apart and rearrange it, suppressing or omitting what he considers unimportant and exaggerating dominant elements.

One principle of native design is that all decorated spaces be filled, so that small figures or purely formal motifs can be added where necessary. The latter device is particularly noticeable on boxes where a face is placed in the center of the panel, and stylized claw, face, eye, joint, and feathers fill in the remaining space.

On totem poles the figures are often telescoped together, folded and shortened, or placed one on the other. Figures are generally carved facing forward. Frog, Whale, and occasionally Beaver are notable exceptions for they often hang head downward. Human figures carved head down indicated either a debtor or a slave and were used to humiliate or disgrace some lineage. The account of the debt owed the pole owners was always made public when the pole was set up.

Since the Forest Service started work on restoring totem poles and other examples of Northwest Coast woodcraft, interest in native American art has been greatly stimulated. Native Americans have been quick to appreciate the effort to preserve their art and have agreed to transfer the poles to central locations where they may be incorporated into national monuments. Master carvers, who learned to carve in their youth, pass the art and the complex, sophisticated symbolism of the rich mythology to the next generation.